# Maggie's Sidekick

by Eve Beck
illustrated by Robbie Short

**Scott Foresman**
**is an imprint of**

Glenview, Illinois • Boston, Massachusetts • Mesa, Arizona
Shoreview, Minnesota • Upper Saddle River, New Jersey

Every effort has been made to secure permission and provide appropriate credit for photographic material. The publisher deeply regrets any omission and pledges to correct errors called to its attention in subsequent editions.

Unless otherwise acknowledged, all photographs are the property of Pearson.

Photo locations denoted as follows: Top (T), Center (C), Bottom (B), Left (L), Right (R), Background (Bkgd)

Illustrations by Robbie Short

Photograph 20 Tom Wagner/Corbis

ISBN 13: 978-0-328-39382-4
ISBN 10: 0-328-39382-7



1 2 3 4 5 6 7 8 9 10 V010 17 16 15 14 13 12 11 10 09 08

Maggie lived with her mother in a very tall apartment building in the city of Chicago. They lived on the ninth floor.

Maggie's father lived in California, and when Maggie had vacations from school, she would fly on an airplane to visit him.

It was October, and Maggie's birthday was a week away. She was going to be eight years old and couldn't wait!

“What do you want for your birthday, Maggie?” Mom asked.

“I want a sidekick,” said Maggie.

“A sidekick?” Mom said, laughing. “What do you mean?”

“Well, I have lots of friends at school, but I don’t have any brothers or sisters… and sometimes you just want a buddy all to yourself,” Maggie said. “How about a dog?”

“We don’t have a yard for a dog,” Mom replied.

“How about a cat?” said Maggie.

“Cats make me sneeze. Would you like a goldfish?” Mom asked.

“Goldfish are nice, and they are pretty to look at, but a goldfish couldn’t really be my sidekick,” Maggie said.

“I see what you mean,” said Mom.

The next week seemed to drag by. Maggie went to school, played with her friends, and did her homework, but all she could think about was her birthday.

On the big day, Maggie woke up bright and early. She rushed into the kitchen where her mother was already awake and making eggs and toast for breakfast.

"Happy birthday, sweetheart!" she exclaimed, giving Maggie a big kiss. Maggie's mother handed her a package from her grandparents. It was a new book by her favorite author and a birthday card. She showed it to her mother.

"That looks like a great book!" Mom said.

"Do you want to open your present from me now or when you get home from school?" Mom asked.

"Can I open it now?" Maggie asked, grinning. Maggie sat and waited, munching her toast while Mom brought in a giant box wrapped in red and white paper with a red bow.

"Here you go!" she said.

Maggie removed the red bow and tore the wrapping paper apart. She lifted the flaps of the cardboard box. In it she found a jumble of metal pieces with an instruction sheet that read: "Construct your own robot!"

Maggie gasped. "A robot!" she cried. "Mom, you really did get me a sidekick!" She started taking the pieces out of the box.

"Maggie, I know you are excited, but you'll have to wait until after school. You are going to miss the bus, and I'm going to be late for work," Mom said.

Maggie threw her arms around her mother's waist and gave her a hug. Then she grabbed her backpack and dashed out the door.

That day at school, Maggie could barely sit still. All she could think about was the robot. At recess she told her friends about her new sidekick.

After school, she raced up the stairs and into the elevator, hopping up and down impatiently as it slowly climbed to the ninth floor.

Her mother was reading on the couch when she burst through the door.

"Hi, Mom," she said, heading directly for the kitchen where the robot was waiting to be assembled.

“Hi, birthday girl,” said Mom, following Maggie. They read the directions and put the metal pieces together until the parts had formed a small metal creature.

“Oh, Mom, thank you! She’s the sidekick I’ve always wanted!” Maggie exclaimed. The final step of the instructions said: “Press the power button and the fun begins!” Maggie and Mom looked at each other and grinned.

“Press the button!” her mother said. Maggie pressed the purple button on the robot’s chest. The robot’s black eyes lit up and her mouth turned up in a smile.

"Hello," the robot said. "I am your robot. What is your name?"

"Wow, you can talk? I'm Maggie. What is your name?" Maggie asked.

"You can give me a name," the robot replied.

"Can I call you Harriet?" Maggie asked the robot, amazed at this great invention.

"Yes, I like that name," the robot Harriet said.

"And will you be my sidekick and play with me?" Maggie asked Harriet.

"Yes, Maggie, I will," said Harriet.

Maggie and Harriet played all evening, except when Maggie's grandparents came over to eat cake and ice cream. When it was time for bed, Maggie's mother made a little bed for Harriet on the floor in Maggie's room.

Maggie's mother told them a bedtime story, tucked them both in, and turned out the light.

"Good night, Harriet," Maggie said. "I'm glad you are my robot."

"Good night, Maggie. I am glad I am your robot too," said Harriet.

The next day after school, Maggie was cleaning her room when she had an idea.

"Will you clean my room, Harriet?"

"Yes, Maggie," said Harriet. Maggie sat on her bed and watched as Harriet put her toys away and hung up her clean clothes.

Later that evening, Maggie was reading her new book when she realized it would be much easier if someone just read it to her.

"Will you read this book to me?" she asked Harriet.

"Yes, Maggie," said Harriet.

"And will you get me a glass of water from the kitchen?" Maggie asked.

"Yes, Maggie," Harriet said.

The rest of the week passed by quickly. Maggie thought about how easy things were when she had someone to do everything for her. Every day when she got home from school, Harriet would be waiting.

"Do you want to play, Maggie?" Harriet would ask.

"Maybe later," Maggie would say. "Would you get me a snack?"

One morning, Maggie's mother came into her room while Harriet was in the living room picking up Maggie's toys.

"Maggie, I thought you wanted a sidekick, not someone to clean up after you," she said.

"Harriet *is* my sidekick!" Maggie exclaimed.

"A sidekick is a friend and a companion, not someone who does everything for you," Maggie's mother said.

"Oh, Mom, Harriet doesn't mind," Maggie said, but she wasn't so sure.

That evening, Harriet didn't bother asking Maggie to play. She brought Maggie her pajamas without being asked, and then went and sat by herself on her little bed.

"Will you bring me some water, Harriet?" Maggie asked.

"Yes, Maggie," Harriet said with a sigh.

Maggie looked up in surprise. She had never heard Harriet sigh before.

"What's wrong, Harriet?" Maggie asked.

"Oh, Maggie," Harriet said. "I have so much fun when we play together, but lately you have not wanted to play at all. I do not mind helping you pick up and get ready for school, but it's boring doing it all by myself. I do not really feel like your sidekick at all."

Maggie felt awful, so she gave Harriet a hug and a kiss on her metal cheek.

"I didn't know that you have the same feelings humans do," she said.

"I am a unique invention," said Harriet. "I am programmed to have feelings like humans."

"Oh, Harriet, I'm so ashamed that I made you do everything for me. All I wanted was a sidekick, but it was so easy to let you do things for me. I forgot how much fun we have when we just play," Maggie said, tears running down her cheeks. "From now on we'll just be friends and play together," Maggie said.

"I would like that, Maggie," Harriet said.

From that day on Harriet was truly Maggie's sidekick and friend. They played games, went for walks, and swung on the playground swings together. Sometimes Harriet would help Maggie with her chores, but Maggie never asked Harriet to do them for her. Each night before they went to bed, they took turns reading to each other.

Before Maggie turned out the lights she would say, "Good night, Harriet, I love you."

And Harriet would say, "Good night, Maggie, I love you too."

# Inventions

Inventions can come from simple ideas. If someone has an idea that they think will be useful for society, such as a robot, they must come up with a model or blueprint of their idea. A blueprint is a picture of something that shows the exact sizes and measurements. Then they have to apply for a patent. A patent is a license that means no one but you can produce your invention.

Do you have any ideas that you think would make good inventions? What are they?

Many people have invented robots—although none of them can do all the things the robot in the story can do.